Overcoming Grief and Trauma

ONE SCRIPTURE AT A TIME

30-DAY JOURNAL

This scripture writing journal belongs to:

_____

Overcoming Grief and Trauma, Scripture Writing Journal

Published by Watersprings Media House, LLC.

P.O. Box 1284

Olive Branch, MS 38654

www.waterspringsmedia.com

© 2018 Copyrights Watersprings Media House. All rights reserved.

No portion of this book may be reproduced, stored in a retrieval system or transmitted in any form or by any means (electronic, mechanical, photocopy, recording, scanning, or other), except for brief quotations in critical reviews of articles, without the prior written permission of the writer.

Scripture quotations credited to NIV are from the Holy Bible, New International Version. Copyright © 1973, 1978, 1984, 2011 by Biblica, Inc. Used by permission. All rights reserved worldwide.

ISBN 13: 978-1-94877-08-4

Introduction

From personal experience, I know that there are many deep emotions that cycle the heart of someone who is grieving and hurting from a traumatic experience. One day may feel like dread and another day may feel like anger or anxiety. The scriptures in this journal spoke to my heart, mind and soul during my personal time of grief, tragedy and loss. I found solice in God's Word and it helped to sustain me from day to day. There were days that started and ended in tears with perhaps a scripture somewhere in between. Opening the Word of God during my darkest days gave me hope and breathed life into me one moment at a time, one day at a time and one scripture at a time.

How to Use this Scripture Writing Journal

As you use this journal, for the next 30 days, your heart will grow stronger and your hope deeper. Hope sustains us and fuels our faith especially during our most difficult days. I encourage you to allow the Spirit of the living God to breathe into you every day. This scripture writing journal provides four sections each day to write from the provided scripture:

Write - As you write the Word of God, allow it to penetrate your heart and mind afresh, even if its a familiar scripture.

Listen - Listen to your heart, good, bad or indifferent and simply write. Then listen to the heart of God through that scripture and/or in that moment and write what you hear or what you understand from that scripture.

Pray - Next, take a moment to reconcile your heart and thoughts with God's words, then write a prayer from your heart. Acknowledge who God is and where you are, thanking and asking God for what you need in that moment.

My Affirmation - I've discovered that speaking positively, declaring and decreeing words of faith and affirmation will encourage you and shift your thinking. At the end of each entry write a personal affirmation. Take it a step further, put in on a post-it note, your cell phone screen or make it your daily hashtag on social media. Speak it and repeat it until you feel a difference in your spirit.

Athena C. Shack
#OVERCOMER

Isaiah 26:3

*You will keep in perfect peace those whose minds
are steadfast, because they trust in you.*

Listen TO THE WORD

Pray the Word

My Affirmation

Psalm 116:2

*Because he turned his ear to me,
I will call on him as long as I live.*

Write the Word

Listen to the Word

Pray the Word

My Affirmation

Psalm 27:13

*I remain confident of this: I will see the goodness
of the LORD in the land of the living.*

Write the Word

Listen to the Word

Pray the Word

My Affirmation

Psalm 118:5

*When hard pressed, I cried to the LORD;
he brought me into a spacious place.*

Write the Word

Listen TO THE WORD

Pray the Word

My Affirmation

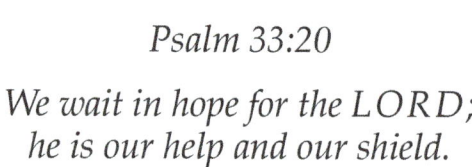

Psalm 33:20

We wait in hope for the LORD;
he is our help and our shield.

Write the Word

Listen to the Word

Pray the Word

My Affirmation

Psalm 69:1

*Save me, O God, for the waters
have come up to my neck.*

Write the Word

Listen to the Word

Pray the Word

My Affirmation

Psalm 126:5

*Those who sow with tears
will reap with songs of joy.*

Write the Word

Listen to the Word

Pray the Word

My Affirmation

Psalm 34:18

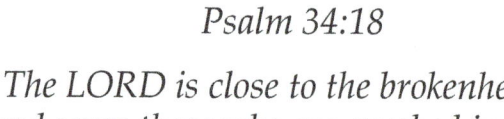
*The LORD is close to the brokenhearted
and saves those who are crushed in spirit.*

Write the Word

Listen to the Word

Pray the Word

My Affirmation

Jeremiah 29:11

*"For I know the plans I have for you,"
declares the LORD, "plans to prosper you and
not to harm you, plans to give you hope and a future.*

Write the Word

Listen to the Word

Pray the Word

My Affirmation

Psalm 118:17

*I will not die but live, and will proclaim
what the LORD has done.*

Write the Word

Listen to the Word

Pray the Word

My Affirmation

Psalm 55:22

*Cast your cares on the LORD and he will sustain you;
he will never let the righteous be shaken.*

Write the Word

Listen to the Word

Pray the Word

My Affirmation

Psalm 34:15

*The eyes of the LORD are on the righteous,
and his ears are attentive to their cry;*

Write the Word

Listen to the Word

Pray the Word

My Affirmation

Psalm 77:1

*I cried out to God for help;
I cried out to God to hear me.*

Write the Word

Listen TO THE WORD

Pray the Word

My Affirmation

Philippians 4:9

*Whatever you have learned or received or
heard from me, or seen in me – put it into practice.
And the God of peace will be with you.*

Write the Word

Listen to the Word

Pray the Word

My Affirmation

Psalm 31:9

Be merciful to me, LORD, for I am in distress; my eyes grow weak with sorrow, my soul and body with grief.

Write the Word

Listen to the Word

Pray the Word

My Affirmation

1 Peter 5:10

And the God of all grace, who called you to his eternal glory in Christ, after you have suffered a little while, will himself restore you and make you strong, firm and steadfast.

Listen to the Word

Pray the Word

My Affirmation

Psalm 130:5

*I wait for the LORD, my whole being waits,
and in his word I put my hope.*

Write the Word

Listen to the Word

Pray the Word

My Affirmation

Psalm 69:15

Do not let the floodwaters engulf me or the depths swallow me up or the pit close its mouth over me.

Write the Word

Listen to the Word

Pray the Word

My Affirmation

1 Peter 5:7

*Cast all your anxiety on him
because he cares for you.*

Write the Word

Listen to the Word

Pray the Word

My Affirmation

Psalm 141:8

*But my eyes are fixed on you, Sovereign LORD;
in you I take refuge – do not give me over to death.*

Write THE WORD

Listen to the Word

Pray the Word

My Affirmation

2 Corinthians 12:9

*But he said to me, "My grace is sufficient for you,
for my power is made perfect in weakness."
Therefore I will boast all the more gladly about
my weaknesses, so that Christ's power may rest on me.*

Write the Word

Listen to the Word

Pray the Word

My Affirmation

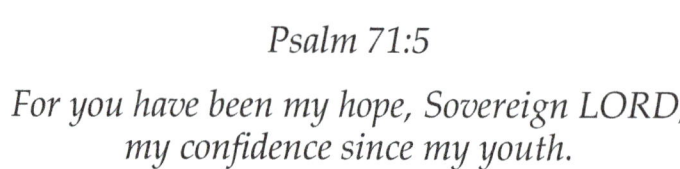

Psalm 71:5

*For you have been my hope, Sovereign LORD,
my confidence since my youth.*

Write the Word

Listen to the Word

Pray the Word

My Affirmation

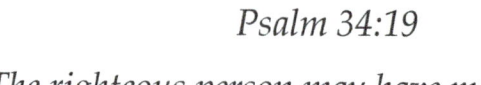

Psalm 34:19

*The righteous person may have many troubles,
but the LORD delivers him from them all;*

Write the Word

Listen to the Word

Pray the Word

My Affirmation

Isaiah 40:31a

*But those who hope in the LORD
will renew their strength...*

Write the Word

Listen to the Word

Pray the Word

My Affirmation

Psalm 22:1

My God, my God, why have you forsaken me? Why are you so far from saving me, so far from my cries of anguish?

Write the Word

Listen TO THE WORD

Pray the Word

My Affirmation

Psalm 147:3

*He heals the brokenhearted
and binds up their wounds.*

Write the Word

Listen to the Word

Pray the Word

My Affirmation

Psalm 56:13

For you have delivered me from death and my feet from stumbling, that I may walk before God in the light of life.

Write the Word

Listen to the Word

Pray the Word

_____

My Affirmation

Psalm 142:5

*I cry to you, LORD; I say, "You are my refuge,
my portion in the land of the living."*

Write the Word

Listen TO THE WORD

Pray the Word

My Affirmation

Romans 15:13

May the God of hope fill you with all joy and peace as you trust in him, so that you may overflow with hope by the power of the Holy Spirit.

Write the Word

Listen to the Word

Pray the Word

My Affirmation

Isaiah 43:19

*See, I am doing a new thing! Now it springs up;
do you not perceive it? I am making a way
in the wilderness and streams in the wasteland.*

Write the Word

Listen to the Word

Pray the Word

My Affirmation

www.ingramcontent.com/pod-product-compliance
Lightning Source LLC
Chambersburg PA
CBHW060043230426
43661CB00004B/641